~A BINGO BOOK~

Minnesota
Bingo Book

COMPLETE BINGO GAME IN A BOOK

Written By Rebecca Stark

ISBN 978-0-87386-516-6

Educational Books 'n' Bingo

Printed in the U.S.A.

DIRECTIONS

INCLUDED:

List of Terms

Templates for Additional Terms and Clues

2 Clues per Term

30 Unique Bingo Cards

Markers

1. **Either cut apart the book or make copies of ALL the sheets. You might want to make an extra copy of the clue sheets to use for introduction and review. Keep the sheets in an envelope for easy reuse.**

2. Cut apart the call cards with terms and clues.

3. Pass out one bingo card per student. There are enough for a class of 30.

4. Pass out markers. You may cut apart the markers included in this book or use any other small items of your choice.

5. Decide whether or not you will require the entire card to be filled. Requiring the entire card to be filled provides a better review. However, if you have a short time to fill, you may prefer to have them do the just the border or some other format. Tell the class before you begin what is required.

6. There are 50 terms. Read the list before you begin. If there are any terms that have not been covered in class, you may want to read to the students the term and clues before you begin.

7. There is a blank space in the middle of each card. You can instruct the students to use it as a free space or you can write in answers to cover terms not included. Of course, in this case you would create your own clues. (Templates provided.)

8. Shuffle the cards and place them in a pile. Two or three clues are provided for each term. If you plan to play the game with the same group more than once, you might want to choose a different clue for each game. If not, you may choose to use more than one clue.

9. Be sure to keep the cards you have used for the present game in a separate pile. When a student calls, "Bingo," he or she will have to verify that the correct answers are on his or her card AND that the markers were placed in response to the proper questions. Pull out the cards that are on the student's card keeping them in the order they were used in the game. Read each clue as it was given and ask the student to identify the correct answer from his or her card.

10. If the student has the correct answers on the card AND has shown that they were marked in response to the *correct questions,* then that student is the winner and the game is over. If the student does not have the correct answers on the card OR he or she marked the answers in response to *the wrong questions,* then the game continues until there is a proper winner.

11. If you want to play again, reshuffle the cards and begin again.

Have fun!

TERMS

Agate

Arrowhead Region

Blueberry (-ies)

Bluff Country

Border(-ed)

Central Lakes

Climate

Common Loon(s)

Crop(s)

County (-ies)

Robert de la Salle
     René-Robert Cavelier, Sieur de la Salle)

Duluth

Eagle Mountain

Executive Branch

Fish (-ing)

Flag

Fort Snelling

Fur

"Hail! Minnesota"

Father Louis Hennepin

Ice Hockey

Industries

Iron

Judicial Branch

Lake(s)

Lake Superior

Legislative Branch

Livestock

Louisiana Purchase

Marquette and Joliet

Mayo Clinic

Minneapolis

Mississippi River

Morel(s)

Motto

Pine

Ojibwe

Pink and White Lady Slipper

Prairieland

Red River

Seal

Sioux

St. Anthony Falls

St. Croix River

St. Paul

Territory (-ies)

Twin Cities

Union

University of Minnesota

Wild Rice

Additional Terms

Choose as many additional terms as you would like and write them in the squares. Repeat each as desired.

Cut out the squares and randomly distribute them to the class.

Instruct the students to place their square on the center space of their card.

Clues for
Additional Terms

Write three clues for each of your additional terms.

_____ 1. 2. 3.	_____ 1. 2. 3.
_____ 1. 2. 3.	_____ 1. 2. 3.
_____ 1. 2. 3.	_____ 1. 2. 3.

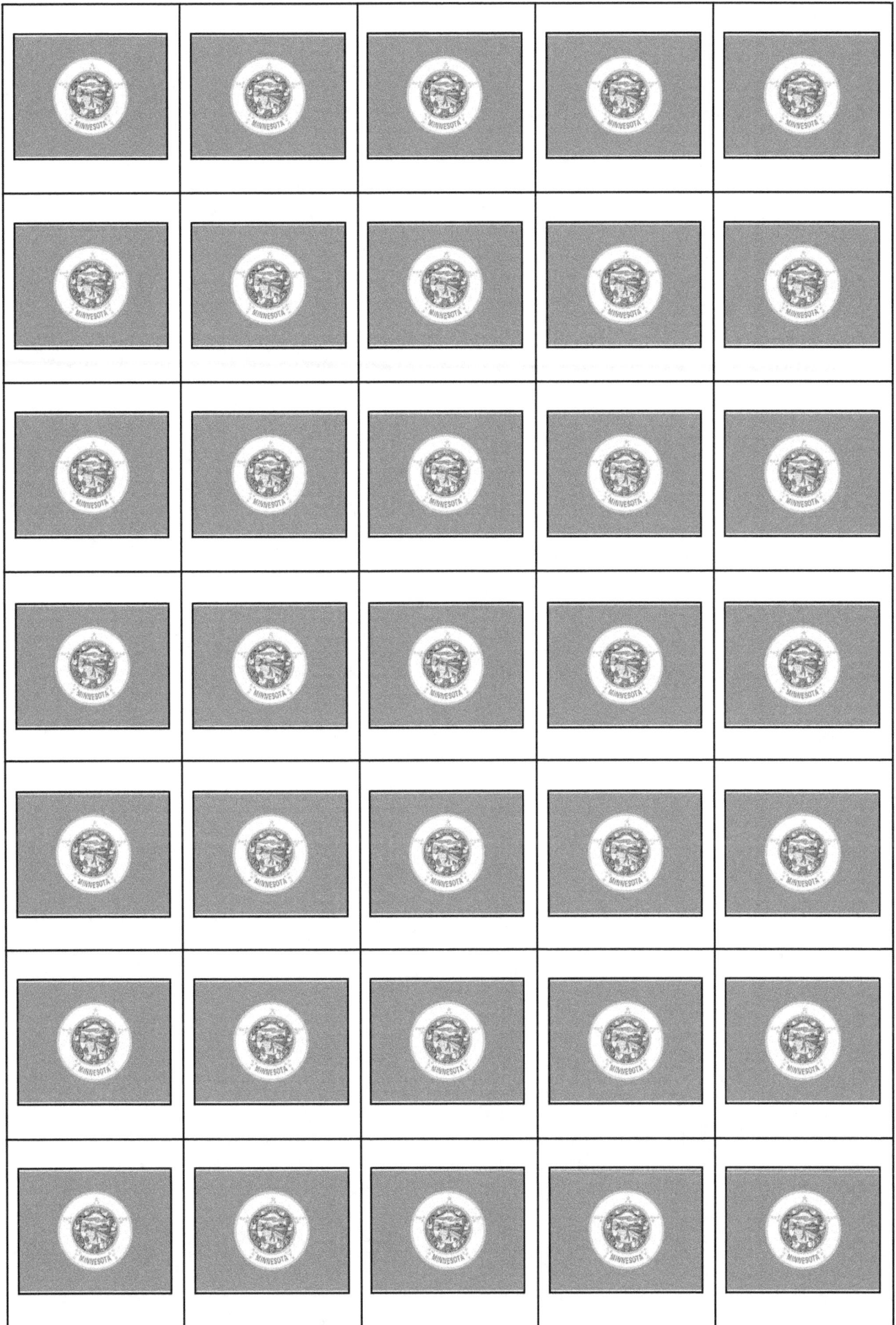

Agate 1. Lake Superior ___ is the state gemstone. 2. Lake Superior ___ is a beautiful quartz stone. It is banded with rich red and orange colors, which it gets from the soil.	**Arrowhead Region** 1. The northeastern part of Minnesota is called the ___ because of its pointed shape. This region borders the Lake Superior North Shore. 2. The rugged ___ of northeastern Minnesota is dotted with thousands of lakes. It includes the Sawtooth Mountains. Ely, Grand Marais, and Duluth are some towns in this region.
Blueberry (-ies) 1. The ___ muffin is the official state muffin. 2. Wild ___ are native to northeastern Minnesota, where they grow in bogs, on hillsides, and in cut-over forested areas.	**Bluff Country** 1. ___ is in southeastern Minnesota. The western edge is mostly flat or mildly rolling farmland. Farther east the landscape becomes more rugged. 2. Forestville Mystery Cave State Park and Great River Bluffs State Park are in this region in southeastern Minnesota.
Border(-ed) 1. These states ___ Minnesota: Iowa, Wisconsin, and South Dakota. 2. Minnesota is ___ on the north by Canada. It is ___ on the east by Lake Superior.	**Central Lakes** 1. The Seven Sisters Prairie, a group of seven glacially-created knolls, is on the north side of Lake Christina in the ___ Region. 2. Brainerd, Detroit Lakes, and Fergus Falls are in the ___ Region.
Climate 1. Minnesota generally has a continental ___, with cold winters and hot summers. 2. Lake Superior has a moderating effect on the ___ of nearby areas. These areas are cooler in the summer and warmer in the winter than most of the state.	**Common Loon(s)** 1. The ___ is the official state bird. It has a distinctive cry. Many migrate to Minnesota in the summer. 2. Although clumsy on land, ___ are strong flyers and excellent underwater swimmers.
Crop(s) 1. Farming is a major industry in the state. Corn for grain, soybeans and wheat are the most valuable cash ___. 2. Leading vegetable ___ are peas, potatoes and sweet corn. Apples are the leading fruit ___ , and the honeycrisp™ apple is the state fruit.	**County (-ies)** 1. Minnesota has 87 ___. 2. Minneapolis is the ___ seat of Hennepin ___, the largest by population.

Robert de la Salle **(René-Robert Cavelier, Sieur de la Salle)** 1. This French explorer was sent by King Louis XIV to travel south from Canada and sail down the Mississippi River to the Gulf of Mexico. 2. The area claimed by ___ for France in 1682 included what is now Minnesota.	**Duluth** 1. ___ has the nation's largest inland harbor. It was named after French soldier and explorer Daniel Greysolon, Sieur du Lhut. 2. ___ forms a metropolitan area with Superior, Wisconsin. The area is called the Twin Ports.
Eagle Mountain 1. At about 2,300 feet above sea level, ___ in Cook County is the highest point in Minnesota. 2. ___, the highest point in the state, is in the Misquah Hills, which are within the Superior National Forest in northeastern Minnesota.	**Executive Branch** 1. The governor is head of the ___. The present-day governor is [fill in]. 2. The ___ of government enforces laws. It comprises the governor, the lieutenant governor, the secretary of state, the attorney general, the state auditor, and several agencies.
Fish(-ing) 1. Commercial and recreational ___ contributes greatly to the state's economy. The walleye pike is the state ___. 2. Minnesota is first nationally in the sales of ___ licenses per capita. Walleye, small-mouth and large-mouth bass, sunfish, perch, and northern pike are among the species caught.	**Flag** 1. The state seal is centered on a medium blue field on the state ___. 2. Nineteen stars are arranged outside the wreath on the state ___. They symbolize the fact that Minnesota was the 19th state to enter the Union *after* the original thirteen, making it the 32nd state.
Fort Snelling 1. This military fortification ___ was completed in 1825. It overlooked the junction of the Minnesota and Mississippi rivers. 2. ___ was one of several forts constructed after the War of 1812 to protect the interests of the United States.	**Fur** 1. In the late1600s, European settlers traded with local Indian tribes for ___. Beaver was the most popular. 2. French-Canadian ___ traders began arriving in Minnesota around 1650, setting up a number of trading posts.
"Hail! Minnesota" 1. ___ is the state song. 2. "Minnesota, hail to thee!" is the first line of ___.	**Father Louis Hennepin** 1. In 1679 ___ sailed with Robert de la Salle from Canada through the Great Lakes aboard *Le Griffon.* 2. ___ explored the area now known as Minnesota. He discovered St. Anthony Falls in 1680.

Minnesota Bingo

Ice Hockey 1. ___ is the official state sport. 2. The Minnesota Wild is a professional ___ team.	**Industries** 1. Farming and mining are important ___. 2. Printing and manufacture of paper products are important ___.
Iron 1. Most of Minnesota's mining income comes from ___ ore. 2. The Mesabi Range is the largest of four major ___ ranges in the region.	**Judicial Branch** 1. The ___ interprets what our laws mean and makes decisions about the laws and those who break them. 2. The ___ has three levels of courts: district courts, the Court of Appeals, and the Supreme Court.
Lake(s) 1. Minnesota has more than 15,000 ___; 11,842 of them cover 10 acres or more. 2. The nickname "Land of 10,000 ___" is on the state quarter.	**Lake Superior** 1. ___ borders Minnesota on the east. Its shore is the lowest point in the state. 2. ___ is the largest freshwater lake in the world by surface area and the third largest by volume.
Legislative Branch 1. The ___ of government comprises the Senate and the House of Representatives. 2. The ___ makes the laws.	**Livestock** 1. Dairy products, hogs, cattle, and turkeys are valuable ___ products. 2. Dairy products are the most important ___ products. Minnesota is a leading producer of milk, most of which is made into butter and cheese.
Louisiana Purchase 1. The ___ doubled the size of the United States and opened up the continent to westward expansion. It included the part of Minnesota west of the Mississippi. 2. The Lewis and Clark Expedition explored the territory west of the Mississippi River that was acquired by the ___ of 1803.	**Marquette and Joliet** 1. This team comprised a Jesuit missionary and a fur trader. They were the first Europeans to explore and map much of the Mississippi River. 2. In 1673 this team explored the unsettled territory from the Great Lakes region to the Gulf of Mexico for France.

Mayo Clinic 1. Rochester is home to the ___, a world-renowned medical center. 2. The ___ developed gradually from the medical practice of a pioneer doctor, Dr. William Worrall Mayo.	**Minneapolis** 1. ___ is the largest city in Minnesota. It is the center of trade in the Midwest. It adjoins St. Paul. 2. From 1880 to 1930, ___ was known as the "Flour Milling Capital of the World." Mill City Museum is in this city.
Mississippi River 1. The ___ begins its 2,350-mile* path to the sea at Lake Itasca. The Red River of the North and the St. Lawrence River also begin in Minnesota. 2. The ___ runs along the southeastern border of the state. *Estimates of the length of the river vary.	**Morel(s)** 1. The ___ is the state mushroom. ___ thrive in the Great Lakes region. 2. These mushrooms are considered a rare delicacy; they are more common in the southeastern part of the state than in the rest of the state.
Motto 1. Minnesota adopted the French phrase "L'Etoile du Nord" as the official state motto in 1861. It appears on the Great Seal. 2. Translated from the French, the state ___ is "The Star of the North."	**Pine** 1. The red ___, commonly known as the Norway ___, is Minnesota's state tree. 2. ___ Island State Forest, located in Koochiching County in northern Minnesota, is the largest of Minnesota's 58 state forests,
Ojibwe 1. The ___, or Chippewa, call themselves the Anishinabe, which means "original person." There are 7 federally recognized ___ tribes in Minnesota. 2. Bois Forte, Fond du Lac, Fond du Lac, Leech Lake, Mille Lacs, Red Lake, and White Earth are ___ reservations in Minnesota.	**Pink and White Lady Slipper** 1. The ___ is the state flower. 2. Since 1925 this rare wildflower has been protected by Minnesota state law.
Prairieland 1. ___ covers southwestern and west-central Minnesota. This region of rolling plains is covered with row crops. 2. The headwaters of the Minnesota River are in the ___ region. Montevideo, Mankato and Luverne are towns in this region. Minnesota Bingo	**Red River** 1. The ___ Valley region is named for the ___ of the North, which flows northward to Canada along the western border of Minnesota. 2. The ___ Valley is on the edge of the great plains. This rich agricultural region was once covered in tall prairie grass. © Barbara M. Peller

Seal 1. The Indian on horseback on the Great ___ represents the Indian heritage of Minnesota. 2. The Great ___ shows a barefoot farmer plowing a field near St. Anthony Falls on the Mississippi River.	**Sioux** 1. Lower Sioux, Prairie Island, Shakopee Mdewakanton, and Upper Sioux are Dakota, or ___ , reservations of Minnesota. 2. The Mystic Lake Casino Hotel is owned by the Shakopee Mdewakanton ___ tribe; it is a popular tourist attraction.
St. Anthony Falls 1. ___ is the only natural major waterfall on the Upper Mississippi River. Father Louis Hennepin discovered ___ in 1680. 2. ___ became the main source of power for the many lumber and flour mills that were built in the area during the 1800s.	**St. Croix River** 1. The lower 125 miles of this 169-mile river form the border between Wisconsin and Minnesota. 2. Marine-On-St. Croix, Afton, Stillwater, and Lovely Taylors Falls are towns in the ___ Valley region.
St. Paul 1. ___ is the capital of Minnesota and the second largest city. 2. ___ lies mostly on the east bank of the Mississippi River near its confluence with the Minnesota River. It adjoins Minneapolis.	**Territory (-ies)** 1. The part of Minnesota east of the Mississippi was included in the Northwest ___ . which was organized under the Northwest Ordinance of 1787. 2. Minnesota was part of Indiana, Michigan, and Wisconsin ___ successively. In 1849 Minnesota was organized as a ___ .
Twin Cities 1. The Minneapolis-Saint Paul metropolitan area is known as the ___ . 2. One of the ___ is the state capital; the other is the largest city. About 60% of the state's residents live in the ___ .	**Union** 1. Minnesota Territory was admitted to the ___ as a state on May 11, 1858. 2. The year 1858 is on the Great Seal; that is the year that Minnesota entered the ___ , becoming the 32nd state.
University of Minnesota 1. The Twin Cities campus of the ___ actually comprises 2 campuses: one in Minneapolis and one in St. Paul. 2. ___ 's athletic teams are known as the Minnesota Golden Gophers.	**Wild Rice** 1. ___ is the state grain. 2. ___ is actually an aquatic grass. It grows mainly in the Great Lakes region.

Minnesota Bingo

Pink and White Lady Slipper	Agate	Blueberry (-ies)	"Hail! Minnesota"	Border(-ed)
Fort Snelling	Arrowhead Region	Union	Marquette and Joliet	Seal
Twin Cities	Louisiana Purchase		Motto	University of Minnesota
Territory (-ies)	Red River	St. Paul	Livestock	Minneapolis
Morel(s)	Industries	Executive Branch	St. Anthony Falls	Lake(s)

Minnesota Bingo

Territory (-ies)	Twin Cities	Judicial Branch	Prairieland	Legislative Branch
Minneapolis	Fish(-ing)	Common Loon(s)	Red River	Mississippi River
County (-ies)	Industries		Iron	St. Paul
Pine	Ojibwe	Louisiana Purchase	Wild Rice	Border(-ed)
Seal	Union	Executive Branch	Fort Snelling	St. Anthony Falls

Minnesota Bingo

Industries	St. Paul	Fish(-ing)	Livestock	Twin Cities
Minneapolis	Arrowhead Region	Crop(s)	Agate	Ice Hockey
Red River	Union		Mississippi River	Bluff Country
Louisiana Purchase	County (-ies)	Morel(s)	Pine	Judicial Branch
St. Anthony Falls	Robert de la Salle	Executive Branch	Wild Rice	Legislative Branch

Minnesota Bingo

Louisiana Purchase	Mississippi River	Blueberry (-ies)	Robert de la Salle	Legislative Branch
Mayo Clinic	Climate	Agate	Prairieland	Twin Cities
Motto	Pine		Lake(s)	"Hail! Minnesota"
St. Paul	Arrowhead Region	Union	Executive Branch	Common Loon(s)
Duluth	Seal	Central Lakes	St. Anthony Falls	University of Minnesota

Minnesota Bingo

Seal	Border(-ed)	Red River	Common Loon(s)	Robert de la Salle
Mayo Clinic	St. Paul	Crop(s)	Iron	Arrowhead Region
Blueberry (-ies)	University of Minnesota		Marquette and Joliet	Father Louis Hennepin
Lake(s)	Legislative Branch	Pink and White Lady Slipper	Wild Rice	Eagle Mountain
Fish(-ing)	Executive Branch	Twin Cities	Louisiana Purchase	Motto

Minnesota Bingo

Bluff Country	Mississippi River	Judicial Branch	Legislative Branch	University of Minnesota
Livestock	Red River	Eagle Mountain	Agate	Twin Cities
Prairieland	Duluth		Climate	Iron
Executive Branch	Morel(s)	Wild Rice	Central Lakes	Blueberry (-ies)
Minneapolis	Common Loon(s)	Pink and White Lady Slipper	Motto	Flag

Minnesota Bingo: Card No. 6

Minnesota Bingo

Pink and White Lady Slipper	Mississippi River	Father Louis Hennepin	St. Paul	Fish(-ing)
Minneapolis	Legislative Branch	Industries	Arrowhead Region	Mayo Clinic
University of Minnesota	"Hail! Minnesota"		Iron	Climate
Louisiana Purchase	Pine	Crop(s)	Territory (-ies)	County (-ies)
Executive Branch	Robert de la Salle	Wild Rice	Central Lakes	Bluff Country

Minnesota Bingo

Motto	Mississippi River	Fur	Livestock	Climate
Mayo Clinic	Blueberry (-ies)	Prairieland	University of Minnesota	Common Loon(s)
Flag	Robert de la Salle		Legislative Branch	Border(-ed)
St. Anthony Falls	Louisiana Purchase	Territory (-ies)	Duluth	Pine
Union	Executive Branch	Central Lakes	Red River	Minneapolis

Minnesota Bingo

Iron	Fish(-ing)	Industries	Flag	Robert de la Salle
Duluth	Legislative Branch	Motto	Red River	Mississippi River
Ice Hockey	Pink and White Lady Slipper		Arrowhead Region	Fur
Eagle Mountain	Border(-ed)	Morel(s)	Marquette and Joliet	Father Louis Hennepin
Pine	Wild Rice	Crop(s)	Territory (-ies)	Lake(s)

Minnesota Bingo: Card No. 9

Minnesota Bingo

Territory (-ies)	Livestock	Climate	Prairieland	Flag
University of Minnesota	Common Loon(s)	Agate	Arrowhead Region	Legislative Branch
Robert de la Salle	Mississippi River		"Hail! Minnesota"	County (-ies)
Morel(s)	Lake(s)	Eagle Mountain	Wild Rice	Ice Hockey
Crop(s)	Minneapolis	Judicial Branch	Seal	Motto

Minnesota Bingo: Card No. 10

Minnesota Bingo

Bluff Country	Mississippi River	Red River	Eagle Mountain	Minneapolis
Fur	Ice Hockey	Marquette and Joliet	Iron	Agate
Mayo Clinic	Legislative Branch		Judicial Branch	Industries
Crop(s)	Twin Cities	Wild Rice	Robert de la Salle	Territory (-ies)
Duluth	Executive Branch	Pink and White Lady Slipper	Central Lakes	Fish(-ing)

Minnesota Bingo

Fish(-ing)	Border(-ed)	Ice Hockey	Livestock	Iron
Industries	Minneapolis	Blueberry (-ies)	Central Lakes	Arrowhead Region
Pink and White Lady Slipper	Father Louis Hennepin		University of Minnesota	Prairieland
Executive Branch	Pine	Legislative Branch	Territory (-ies)	Mayo Clinic
Mississippi River	Fur	Robert de la Salle	Duluth	Common Loon(s)

Minnesota Bingo

Eagle Mountain	Border(-ed)	Bluff Country	Ice Hockey	University of Minnesota
Blueberry (-ies)	Fur	Legislative Branch	Iron	County (-ies)
Livestock	Common Loon(s)		Industries	Father Louis Hennepin
Motto	Wild Rice	Climate	Robert de la Salle	Territory (-ies)
Executive Branch	Lake(s)	Central Lakes	Pink and White Lady Slipper	Marquette and Joliet

Minnesota Bingo: Card No. 13

Minnesota Bingo

Fort Snelling	Legislative Branch	Red River	Iron	Duluth
Common Loon(s)	Pink and White Lady Slipper	Ice Hockey	Arrowhead Region	Mississippi River
Eagle Mountain	"Hail! Minnesota"		Judicial Branch	Crop(s)
Lake(s)	Wild Rice	Robert de la Salle	Climate	Bluff Country
Executive Branch	Prairieland	County (-ies)	Minneapolis	Motto

Minnesota Bingo

Marquette and Joliet	Iron	Red River	Fish(-ing)	Livestock
Bluff Country	Judicial Branch	Agate	Blueberry (-ies)	Duluth
University of Minnesota	Pink and White Lady Slipper		Twin Cities	Mississippi River
Executive Branch	Ice Hockey	Fur	Wild Rice	Eagle Mountain
Minneapolis	Pine	Central Lakes	Flag	Industries

Minnesota Bingo

Climate	Ice Hockey	Fur	Flag	Ojibwe
Prairieland	County (-ies)	Father Louis Hennepin	Mayo Clinic	"Hail! Minnesota"
Eagle Mountain	Border(-ed)		University of Minnesota	Industries
Louisiana Purchase	Common Loon(s)	Executive Branch	Marquette and Joliet	Territory (-ies)
Duluth	St. Croix River	Central Lakes	Pine	Mississippi River

Minnesota Bingo

Crop(s)	Sioux	Lake Superior	Ice Hockey	Fort Snelling
Marquette and Joliet	Duluth	Wild Rice	"Hail! Minnesota"	Father Louis Hennepin
Iron	Motto		St. Croix River	Fur
Lake(s)	Minneapolis	Territory (-ies)	Red River	County (-ies)
Morel(s)	Eagle Mountain	Fish(-ing)	Livestock	Border(-ed)

Minnesota Bingo: Card No. 17

Minnesota Bingo

Flag	Robert de la Salle	Common Loon(s)	Eagle Mountain	Prairieland
Mississippi River	Crop(s)	Morel(s)	University of Minnesota	Duluth
Iron	County (-ies)		Lake Superior	Blueberry (-ies)
Border(-ed)	Agate	Wild Rice	Territory (-ies)	Judicial Branch
St. Croix River	Ice Hockey	Red River	Sioux	Bluff Country

Minnesota Bingo

University of Minnesota	Bluff Country	Ice Hockey	Fur	Territory (-ies)
Marquette and Joliet	Livestock	Mississippi River	Fish(-ing)	"Hail! Minnesota"
Sioux	Robert de la Salle		Arrowhead Region	Twin Cities
Judicial Branch	St. Croix River	Morel(s)	Pine	Lake Superior
Blueberry (-ies)	Ojibwe	Minneapolis	Motto	Central Lakes

Minnesota Bingo

Fort Snelling	Sioux	Livestock	Ice Hockey	Central Lakes
Common Loon(s)	Industries	Mayo Clinic	Morel(s)	Prairieland
Border(-ed)	Father Louis Hennepin		Louisiana Purchase	Agate
Seal	Union	St. Anthony Falls	Pine	St. Croix River
St. Paul	Motto	Ojibwe	Territory (-ies)	Lake Superior

Minnesota Bingo

Marquette and Joliet	Bluff Country	Mayo Clinic	Ice Hockey	Seal
Border(-ed)	Lake Superior	Climate	Fur	Pink and White Lady Slipper
County (-ies)	Minneapolis		Sioux	Red River
Morel(s)	Fish(-ing)	St. Croix River	Lake(s)	Motto
Louisiana Purchase	Ojibwe	Central Lakes	Crop(s)	Pine

Minnesota Bingo

Flag	Judicial Branch	Lake Superior	Blueberry (-ies)	Eagle Mountain
Prairieland	Livestock	Twin Cities	Fur	Arrowhead Region
Common Loon(s)	"Hail! Minnesota"		Pink and White Lady Slipper	Father Louis Hennepin
St. Croix River	Lake(s)	Pine	Agate	Mayo Clinic
Ojibwe	Crop(s)	Sioux	County (-ies)	Louisiana Purchase

Minnesota Bingo: Card No. 22

Minnesota Bingo

Climate	Sioux	Fish(-ing)	Blueberry (-ies)	Central Lakes
Bluff Country	Fort Snelling	Minneapolis	Marquette and Joliet	Agate
Judicial Branch	Eagle Mountain		St. Anthony Falls	Pink and White Lady Slipper
County (-ies)	Ojibwe	St. Croix River	Crop(s)	Pine
Seal	Union	Motto	Morel(s)	Lake Superior

Minnesota Bingo

Climate	Motto	Fort Snelling	Sioux	Fur
Lake Superior	Central Lakes	Mayo Clinic	Prairieland	Pink and White Lady Slipper
Father Louis Hennepin	Flag		Eagle Mountain	County (-ies)
Seal	St. Anthony Falls	St. Croix River	Crop(s)	Border(-ed)
St. Paul	Louisiana Purchase	Ojibwe	Livestock	Union

Minnesota Bingo

Louisiana Purchase	Mayo Clinic	Sioux	Red River	Lake Superior
Agate	Border(-ed)	Marquette and Joliet	Climate	Arrowhead Region
Lake(s)	Fur		St. Anthony Falls	St. Croix River
Twin Cities	Seal	Union	Ojibwe	"Hail! Minnesota"
Central Lakes	Fort Snelling	Common Loon(s)	Duluth	St. Paul

Minnesota Bingo

Lake Superior	Sioux	Judicial Branch	Prairieland	Flag
Morel(s)	Livestock	Fur	Fort Snelling	Climate
Lake(s)	St. Anthony Falls		"Hail! Minnesota"	Louisiana Purchase
Crop(s)	Blueberry (-ies)	Seal	Ojibwe	St. Croix River
Father Louis Hennepin	Duluth	Red River	Union	St. Paul

Minnesota Bingo

Judicial Branch	Common Loon(s)	Sioux	Fort Snelling	Industries
Seal	St. Anthony Falls	Marquette and Joliet	St. Croix River	Arrowhead Region
Wild Rice	Union		Ojibwe	Louisiana Purchase
Flag	Bluff Country	Mayo Clinic	St. Paul	Agate
Duluth	"Hail! Minnesota"	Lake Superior	Twin Cities	Father Louis Hennepin

Minnesota Bingo: Card No. 27

Minnesota Bingo

Judicial Branch	Fort Snelling	Twin Cities	Sioux	Climate
Industries	Lake Superior	St. Anthony Falls	Prairieland	"Hail! Minnesota"
Union	County (-ies)		Father Louis Hennepin	Morel(s)
Territory (-ies)	Flag	Minneapolis	Ojibwe	St. Croix River
Blueberry (-ies)	Iron	Duluth	St. Paul	Seal

Minnesota Bingo

Lake Superior	Fort Snelling	Flag	Marquette and Joliet	Iron
Pine	Morel(s)	Mayo Clinic	Father Louis Hennepin	Twin Cities
Lake(s)	St. Anthony Falls		Arrowhead Region	Sioux
Industries	Seal	Legislative Branch	Ojibwe	St. Croix River
Climate	Fur	St. Paul	Bluff Country	Union

Minnesota Bingo

Robert de la Salle	Sioux	Prairieland	Iron	St. Croix River
Agate	Fort Snelling	Judicial Branch	"Hail! Minnesota"	Arrowhead Region
Lake(s)	Eagle Mountain		Father Louis Hennepin	Mayo Clinic
St. Paul	Bluff Country	Blueberry (-ies)	Ojibwe	St. Anthony Falls
Seal	University of Minnesota	Union	Lake Superior	Twin Cities

Minnesota Bingo: Card No. 30